Prisoner's Lawyers Can Save The American Economy

Make A Buck Doing It & Be Thanked!

Rev. Mike Wanner

Table Of Contents

Introduction

I invite every reader to consider the ideas that can create freedom for taxpayers from the extreme costs of imprisoning huge numbers of our fellow citizens. We have taken for granted that we somehow can afford these costs.

Alas and unfortunately, the costs of incarceration are about to eat up the quality of the American Dream. We are all gradually being banished to involuntary servitude to our insecurities.

Yes, we are threatened by great evil in the world. There is no need for us to overreact. There is some justification for the restrictions that are imposed upon those who have been convicted of a crime.

As taxpayers, we in the greater community have an interest in how our tax dollars are spent. Incarceration is a huge expense and if there were unlimited funds in our national budgets there would be no need to consider changing anything unless fairness was a prominent goal.

Unfortunately, national budgets around the world are stretched by government expenditures and it may make sense for us to evaluate the reasonableness of our expenses. We could find there are little opportunities for prudence.

I previously wrote a book called Prison Possibilities Voluntary Exile as one potential Remedy for our prison problem. This book is a continuation of ideas toward implementing that concept and more.

1 - Why I am Writing This Book

I hope that this book continues the work started by my other books and continues to enhance the lives of Prison Employees, Prisoners, Taxpayers and the Families of Each of these groups?

As I have been writing these books on the subject of Prisons, the complexity of the process has been amazing to me.

The books that I have published so far about the prison situation are:

1. *Angel Raphael Speaks Volume 4: Angels, Addicts, Alcoholics & Prisoners – Oh Yeah!*
2. *Angel Raphael Speaks Volume 5:* Prisoners Caring for Alcoholics - Australia In Miniature Projects Intro
3. *Angel Raphael Speaks Volume 6:* Prisoners Caring for Addicts - Australia In Miniature For Addicts
4. *Prison Jobs Now: Providing Care For Addicts And   Alcoholics*
5. *Angel Raphael Speaks - Prisons* (A Kindle only book -2013)
6. *Contained Care Communities Concept*
7. *Australia In Miniature*
8. *Prison Possibilities Dialogue Series: Concept*
9. *Prison Possibilities Dialogue Series: Volume 2 Dialogues*
10. *Prison Possibilities Dialogue Series: Volume 3 Dialogues*
11. *Prison Possibilities Dialogue Series: Volume 4 Dialogues*
12. *Prison Possibilities Dialogue Series: Volume 5 Dialogues*
13. *Prison Possibilities Voluntary Exile: Concept*
14. *Prison Possibilities Correction Coaches: Concept*
15. *Prison Possibilities for Mexicans: Is A Boat Better than A Wall?*
16. *Prison Possibilities Family Time:* A Reason to Thrive!
17. Prison Genius Pool: *"So Much Genius In Jail"*

2 - The Violent Incarcerated

A large problem for the prisons is the never ending costs and complications of those who have been convicted of a Violent Crime and been given a sentence of Life Imprisonment. The costs do not end.

So Why Am I Inviting Lawyers

The Prison situation is complex and skills are needed. The multiple jurisdictions make analysis difficult and if you try to read up on any aspect of the complexity, you will quickly see that the list of exceptions to anything that looks like a rule is long and laden with specificity. Let's hope the lawyers can work through the complexity.

Disclaimer

I, the author, am not involved with prisons or prisoners but I have talked to many during Hospital Visitations. I am sharing what is coming to me in an effort to spread understanding and trigger conversation that can be helpful. It may be that the discussion needs finessing and I invite your wisdom in the mix.

My guidance has suggested that a lot can be done. I will detail the ramp up to what I have called Voluntary Exile and other ideas that I have shared. Lawyers have the tools to help many people and it would be great if we could motivate them to do it.

3 - Lawyers Can Save Us From Bankruptcy

The legal system is very complicated and the criminal law system has many complicating factors. Unfortunately, there are many people who get incarcerated even though their great lawyers may try their best.

One serious reason for the end of legal efforts to save their client is when the client is ruled guilty by a jury of their peers. When all hope is lost, the lawyers service is terminated and the client goes to prison.

While that may be an end for the courts, the cost of the imprisonment goes on and on and robs our nation of resources that could be used elsewhere. This hurts the citizens of the nation as many things that could be offered to the young and the old and all in between are simply denied because it is unrealistic to find any available funds.

So many criminals sit and rot in jail and we pay and pay and pay and pay. I for one am tired of the limitations that places on my country.

The Angel of Healing - Raphael has been in my awareness, whether real, inspired or imagined, for the last four years and I have resisted following some of the guidance that came to me. I continued to listen and write down the channeled messages.

Within the first forty messages were some fourteen messages about Prisons that came through after a prison minister from Circle of Miracles Ministry called to consult with me about something. All of a sudden, the channeling changed a bit and in message sets 8,9,10 and 11 there were messages about prison interspersed with the general messages.

I later published the fourteen prison messages in a tiny Kindle book called *Angel Raphael Speaks - Prisons*. After that I published nine of the first ten message sets including the contents of the single topic prison set in a paperback titled *Angel Raphael Speaks Volume 1: Take Courage! God Has Healing in Store for You!*

Volume 2 and 3 followed as did The Veterans Healing Six Pack, The PTSD Power Pack, Emergency Medical Kindness Books, Children's Books, Reiki Books, Spiritual Healing Books, Non-Profit Support and many more. I have given away thousands and thousands on Kindle. That is why I wrote the Book *God Bless Kindle & Amazon: Your Message To The World.*

After a dozen years of doing hospital ministry, in 2016 my attention was drawn deeper in to the drug and alcohol crises that are damaging our people and our nation. The *Angels Are Always Around Addicts And Alcoholics* series books followed.

From those books, I was drawn back to the prison awareness and that started all the books mentioned above.

4 - Prisons Situations Are Very Complex

A lot of fingers are pointing around the prison situation but I like it best when any of the fingers point to progress. Like so many things in life, humans react to the obvious choices between apparent good and apparent evil. Things are just not that simple.

There are many choices in between the obvious positions that could have positive possibilities. An absolute path could limit choices. Please dig in to choose wisely.

The book that was a breakthrough for me was *Angel Raphael Speaks Volume 4: Angels, Addicts, Alcoholics & Prisoners – Oh Yeah!*

Raphael was there in spirit as usual but it was me interpreting and integrating so much from different aspects of my spiritual experience and physical life. Putting the pieces of an idea together when I only had some pieces to start was tough but I was not alone and idea flow showed up in the writing process.

Sometimes my head was very surprised what my fingers had typed. It was different than channeling but inside the same family.

Within what I called the Wrapup, there was truth that surprised me. "Once upon a time. England had a great problem with prisoners like we do now. England banished them to a foreign land where these unwanted people created a great land of their own and now the Queen visits them."

We are not Australia but we can learn from them and *Angel Raphael Speaks Volume 4* starts that conversation.

Great strides are being made in reforming a lot of the imbalances that exist within the prison system. I salute the many awesome people who are inviting freedom for those who deserve it and justice for those who have received less than optimal attention. 501C3 organizations need support to function so if there is one you like, remember them at donation time.

The area that will not be quickly remedied by well intentioned organizations is the violent offenders who are in jail for life. These are the people who continue to eat the food that could have helped starving children in the big cities.

My Voluntary Exile book offered a goal bud did not offer any process to facilitate a way to get exiled. I hope that now I can offer some ideas that Lawyers could develop to encourage the jurisprudence system to adopt a path that might help.

The steps are rather simple:
1. Determine Skills That Prisoners might have that could help lesser developed countries.
2. Determine if there are any prisoners who have multiple citizenship that might help them to be more able to find a country that might embrace them.
3. Suggest criteria that could help the idea.

5 - Determining Skills

Determining skills could be difficult and expensive or it could be simple and economical. I would encourage the latter and the recommended procedure would be to try to consider a universal resource that the whole system could use.

Lawyers could make a case for forms that could capture the information needed in standard practice and also when prisoners desire and determine that they would like to participate. Important information to capture would be prisoner's aptitudes and skill sets that could be useful in placement. Education would be very important to record.

In *Prison Possibilities Dialogue Series: Volume 3 Dialogues,* I proposed a business enterprise be created to write, post and share prisoner profiles so that people outside the prison system could shop for skills within the system of prisoners who were looking for skills that prisoners had.

That type of service could be particularly useful for international individuals who needed to access talent but lacked the resources to hire from the international community of skill holders.

Prisoner profile formats could vary from bureau to bureau but they could at least consider including:
　　1. Credit Report
　　2. Educational Report
　　3. Criminal Record
　　4. Skills and Certifications

5. Family History and obligations.
6. Children and spouses
7. Prisoner performance during incarceration
8. Any Violence History

I will post Dialogue 26 "Prison Profile Bureaus" from *Prison Possibilities Dialogue Series: Volume 3 Dialogues* in the next Chapter.

6 - "Prisoner Profile Bureaus
[Dialogue 26]

A New Business Opportunity may be to create a Prisoner Profile Bureau if that is legal and proper to do so. Check out the legality first.

The idea is that many prisoners could benefit from the availability of a publicly available profile on as many aspects of their life as make sense for potential employers. What kind of products to create and who should pay for them are not my concern at this time but the value of such a service could be big.

This idea would only be successful if the orchestrator of the process has sufficient credibility to present themselves to the public as an objective credible resource. My thinking is that this could be a sideline for credit bureaus or it could be a government service or government subsidized service to increase the likelihood that those discharged can stay out. Family status could help to show that the one discharged has the motivation to do a good and credible job.

Skills and capabilities and certifications can help to target an audience for the bureau and increase the value of profiles for the one discharged. The intent of the service would be to qualify great candidates for great companies so that the prisoner can find a great job and the employer a great and long lasting employee. In that process, the community can have more productivity, less prisoners, more workers and less prison costs."

13

7 - Prisoner Exiles

The underlying reality is that the value of a candidate for exile must be enough for the country that beckons them to want them enough to put up with the political negotiations. A completed exile could be a big game of chess or a major accomplishment.

The termination of citizenship would leave the exiled prisoner totally at the mercy of the new country but that could be awesome also for the exiled one. The appeal for the US is the freedom from the legal responsibilities of supervising, feeding, housing, caring for and protecting the exiled one.

The appeal for the exiled one would be new or renewed freedoms to go many places in the world with the exception of the United States. Lawyers for both sides would need to be very specific so that all parties are protected on paper from all obvious and consequential potentials.

I think it can make a lot of Dollars and Cents and Sense for the Federal Government and or the states. I think it can make a lot of sense for the ones exiled also.

The value also needs to be there for the receiving country and the lawyers that put everything together. A big key for the attorneys is probably related to having the clerical work be incorporated in to the system at the earlier defense levels or in the prisoner residency.

8 - No Cancellation

The circumstances of the exile should be clear to all parties that there is to be joint and several termination of all past, present and future connection and access to the United States of America, the various states and all territories.

Agencies should be involved to the degree necessary to insure that all business matters are finished and terminated forever before the exile is complete.

There will never be another US passport issued to the exiled one.

There will never be another US Visa issued to the exiled one.

There will never be another right of US entry of any kind for the exiled one.

9 - Declarations To Be Considered For Both Countries

1. The Nationality of the Exiled One.
   - US – Revocation of Citizenship
   - The Accepting nation – Declaration of Citizenship

2. Declaration of Citizenship Surrender.
   - US – Declaration of Revocation
   - The Accepting nation – Declaration of US Revocation and their Acceptance

3. Clearance by all agencies.
   - US - Clearance of All Government Obligations at all levels of Local, Regional and Federal government
   - The Accepting nation – Specification of Acceptance Terms & The Un-revocable Awareness

4. Final Documentation and Details Needed.
   - US - Termination Effective Date and Time
   - The Accepting nation – Declaration of Citizenship

10 - Why Would A Lawyer Do This?

I hope that we all can realize that Lawyers are business professionals who are endeavoring to provide for their families and provide a good value for their customers. As lawyers they need to work within the existing legal system and so they are capped a bit by the limits of the current system.

Lawyers are also friends of the court and they have the ability to bring forward proposals that are appropriate for the wellbeing of the Nation. Nothing is more important to the nation than solvency.

The sophistication of legal experts allows them to see through the limited legal now and propose skillfully crafted proposals that document ideas that could create new realities with the stroke of the pen. I am not equipped to detail the components of the plans that would be necessary to cut the Red Tape in any of the multiplicity of jurisdictions and circumstances that incarcerate so many people.

My proposal is simply that the nation begin to entertain the feasibility of saving money be revisiting the antiquated and oppressive and complicated laws that exist. The goal of the visitation is to reduce incarceration and the costs thereof.

Even small numbers of prisoner reductions could do great good for the American National bottom line. And this is especially true when the ones exiled are serving life terms that continue to drain the American Economy.

11 - Step One - Realignment

Every Judge, Lawyer, Politician and Government Agency could be invited to make administrative adjustments that would be helpful to this process and be a prudent expense of their normal business or position. 2.3 million (2,300,000)people know a lot about a lot of things that the rest of us know nothing about.

The obvious targeted prisoners would be ones who have professional knowledge. I do not recommend that the candidates be limited to the Professionals, Academicians, High Technology educated persons, trades people, mechanics, administrators, maintenance personnel and computers whizzes.

Many High school dropouts can be much better educated than the poor citizens of many nations. Someone that may seem unemployable here may be a leader in a lesser developed country and may rise to a level of excellence and position that they could never have here.

The idea is to put people where they can have purpose and quality of life and be off the American dole.

12 - Step Two - Plan For Lawyers to get Paid

The Term "Pro Bono" or "For The Good" is a term that lawyers are familiar with but it will not help pay their mortgages or buy them lunch. For this to be successful, there will need to be funding for the lawyer's successes. To be Paid to do "Pro Bono Work for America" could be awesome.

I propose a variety of plans depending on the value of the Human Asset to be determined by these criteria:

1. The Anxiousness of the Prisoner to exit and the ability to self-pay for excellent representation.

2. The Saving value of the exiled prisoner exiting the facility that was holding the prisoner.

3. The Capability Value of the prisoner for the purposes of the receiving nation.

4. Percentage allocation of any of the plans above.

5. Contingency based on savings over time annually.

6. Contingency based on successful performance of prisoner over time.

13 - Public Service Kicker

Additional public value and life saving can be attained by the employment of prisoners while still in jail as advocates for their prisoner colleagues to do a lot of the preparatory case work. This work can help the prisoners meet and work with people wo could be advantageous later.

The engagement of prisoners could be very key to creating a path for graduation from prison and a footing that can help keep that graduate from return to prison school. Saving a life could be an awesome reward for lawyers who participate.

The real powerhouse for the whole system is that possibilities are returned to the consciousness of those who might otherwise be willing to cause trouble and hurt people while incarcerated.

A new term could be created in the prison system that we could call "Collateral Positivity". It could be the polar opposite of the collateral consequences that so often hurt the quality of life for staffers, prisoners and all their families.

Chapter 14 that follows is a direct quote from Message Set 9 of the Angel Raphael Speaks Series which was published in *Angel Raphael Speaks Volume One* and *Angel Raphael Speaks - Prisons* .

14 – "Prison Life of the Future

The complexity of your prison systems is detrimental to many that occupy, serve, visit, and guard them. There is a palpable intensity of negativity present at most facilities.

When one can change their mind, they can change their reality. Could it be that your society could realign prison life to contain the expansion of the need for more prisons.

Unions should not worry as there is no suggestion that these places can be eliminated any time in upcoming centuries. Union leaders could help serve their members by helping the institutions become more user-friendly and economical for all.

The word economical was included to get the attention of the administrators but the goal is really to promote the lessening of dehumanization that exists within the societal dynamics from which the crop of criminals grows. The guarda and others who work for institutions are exposed to the negative energy of the collected criminals and that is not exactly a nurturing vibration.

Please consider as if the vibration of a prison existed on a scale that you could read called the love fear continuum. Consider that a single increment move on that scale that went away from fear and moved towards love was actually beneficial to all who passed through the premises.

As you ever so slightly held that thought, you entertained the possibility for a shift for the imprisoned and guards of the future. Congratulations, for you have allowed some light to shine on a subject that is almost perpetually locked in pessimism." "ARS 9

14 - What Would A Lawyer Need To Do

Depending on the jurisdiction that you practice in and your special skills and connections, plan a meeting and draft some introductory efforts. Things you might want to consider could be:

1. Proposal to Consider Cost Savings for prisoners at

_____ _____.

2. Proposal To Inventory the skills of Prisoners with release dates scheduled between _____ and _____ at _____.

3. Proposal To Inventory the skills of Prisoners who would like to be registered for potential employers and agencies.

4. Hosting a webpage for Prisoners to publicly display their profiles and contact information.

5. Propose to your national associations that they champion enabling efforts for the process of enabling exiles.

While the above may not be implementable real fast, proposals could be deliberately short to avoid misinterpretation and over reaction. Seeds planted once can bear fruit forever. Thank you for reading this far.

For
Considering
These
Ideas

Ever

It Does Not Help Prayer Still Does!

17 - Resource List

Distant Healing Sessions (or Join Mail List) – Write To mikewann@voicenet.com

Books by Rev. Mike at www.Amazon.com

Veterans Healing Six Pack
1. *Trauma Healing Options for VA Hospitals: Help for Veterans to Own Their Healing and their future.*
2. *Trauma Healing Action Steps for Veterans: Help to Start Healing*
3. *Trauma Healing Action Steps for Veterans: Empowerment*
4. *Trauma Healing Action Steps for Veterans: Forgiveness*
5. *Trauma Healing Action Steps for Veterans: Thought Freedom*
6. *Tea For Veterans: Welcome One Home*

PTSD Power Pack:
1. *The PTSD Project: Turn Pain To Power*
2. *PTSD & Soul Retrieval: Putting One Back Together*
3. *PTSD & The Purple PAD: Calling all Scientists and PTSD Patients*

Angel Raphael Speaks Volume 1: Take Courage! God Has Healing in Store for You!
Angel Raphael Speaks Volume 2: Take Courage! God Has Healing in Store for You!
Angel Raphael Speaks Volume 3: Take Courage! God Has Healing in Store for You!
Angel Raphael Speaks Volume 4: Angels, Addicts, Alcoholics & Prisoners – Oh Yeah!
Angel Raphael Speaks Volume 5: Prisoners Caring for Alcoholics - Australia In Miniature Projects Intro
Angel Raphael Speaks Volume 6: Prisoners Caring for Addicts - Australia In Miniature For Addicts
Reiki Journaling from Japan
Reiki Is Alive: God's Great Gift
Four Parts to Healing

Distant Healing: We Are All Connected
Stress Release Energy Work: How To Cope
Does Reiki Love Heal Cancer?
Group Consciousness
Salute To Philadelphia VA Medical Center: Thank You
Reiki Transcript for Reiki 2 & 3 Channels: Dr. Usui Is That You?
God Bless Kindle & Amazon
Puppies Are Different From People
If Your Dog Dies
Toy Guns Are Obsolete
Great Spirit Made Children With Red Skin: AND
The Cage of Fear: Is Not Locked
God Made Children Red, Yellow, Brown, Black & White: Greet Each Child With Kindness
Emergency Medical Kindness In The Cradle Of Liberty: Big City – Cracked Bell
Angels Are Always Around Addicts and Addicts: Help Is Near Now! Invite It In!
Angels Are Always Around Addicts and Alcoholics: Volume 2 - Tools To Help Re-Light Your Life
Prison Jobs Now: Providing Care For Addicts And Addicts
Controlled Care Communities Concept
Australia In Miniature Projects
Prison Possibilities Dialogue Series: Concept
Prison Possibilities Dialogue Series: Volume 2, 3, 4, 5 Dialogues
Prison Possibilities Voluntary Exile
Prison Possibilities Corrections Coaches
Prison Possibilities For Mexicans: Is A Boat Better Than A Wall?
Prison Possibilities Family Time: A Reason to Thrive!
Prison Genius Pool: *"So Much Genius In Jail"*

Little Books at Kindle.com by Rev. Mike:
English Medical History Questionnaire For Non-English Speakers
English Language Helper For Non-English Speakers
Wise Wonderful Women Are The Well Of The Family
Answers for Test & Research: Dowsing Power

Crisis? Reiki! Baby? Reiki!
Bible References For Healing
Angel Raphael Speaks – Prisons
Angel Raphael Speaks – Veterans
The Saint Off Interstate 95

Angel Raphael Speaks through Rev. Mike Wanner. Please visit
http://www.AngelRaphaelSpeaks.com

18 - Angels Please Prayers

Addict's

Angels of Healing Selected
Help Me to Stay Directed
Come To Me From The Sky
I Am Ready to Succeed Not Try
If I Don't Invite You In
I Might Not Win
I Have Been Lost For Too Long
Help Me To Stay Strong

&

Alcoholic's

Angels of Healing On High
Help Me to Stay Dry
Come To Me From The Sky
I Am Ready to Succeed Not Try
If I Don't Invite You In
I Might Not Win
I Have Been Lost For Too Long
Help Me To Stay Strong

From

ANGELS ARE ALWAYS
AROUND ADDICTS
AND ALCOHOLICS

HELP IS NEAR NOW!
INVITE IT IN!

REVEREND
MIKE WANNER

http://AngelRaphaelSpeaks.com/AAAAAAA/

19 - Private Channeling

Angel Raphael Speaks is a series of free messages that are channeled through Reverend Mike Wanner for the Highest good and Highest Healing of all concerned.

Many questions arise about Reverend Mike doing private channeling and he does help with that so e-mail him.

Reverend Mike is available world-wide as a psychic channel, emotional release facilitator, spiritual energy practitioner & teacher, and public speaker. He looks forward to meeting you soon!

Email - mikewann@voicenet.com 215-342-1270

PRIVATE SPIRITUAL READINGS/channelings or Spiritual Healing Sessions: Telephone or in person. Rev. Mike is available for private, one-on-one intuitive sessions with you, his Guide Family, and your Guides. He helps by offering clarity on emotional situations about your life, your purpose, your spirituality, and the release of stuffed emotions and cellular memory.

Connect to the love of your Guides today!
Contact Rev. Mike for an appointment.

Sessions available:

Spiritual Readings
Angel Channeling
Distant Reiki Healing
Distant Clearing of Stuffed Emotions
Distant Clearing Cellular Memory
Distant Clearing Energy Blockages
Distant Clearing of the Chakras
Customized needs
Mastermind dowsing responses to yes/no direction finding questions.

Rev. Mike is a facilitator of healing. He brings you and the Divine together so that you can align with the Divine and have a great time and a great life. All healing is between you and God, as it should be. Go ahead and start without Rev. Mike. Visit his prayer site http://www.Create-A-Prayer.com. Take the first step NOW.

20 - Reverend Mike Wanner

Rev. Mike Wanner started his metaphysical and ministerial studies with Reiki in 1993 and has studied seven styles of Reiki in the U.S., Japan, Canada, Denmark and Australia. He is certified to teach. He became certified to teach Integrated Energy Therapy in 1999 and co-taught the first IET class of the new Millennium. Mike began dowsing in 2001.

Ordained as a Metaphysical Minister of the International Metaphysical Ministry and an Interfaith Minister of the Circle of Miracles Ministry, Rev. Mike practices and teaches spiritual energy therapies in the Philadelphia Area.

Rev. Mike holds ministerial degrees from the University of Metaphysics and the University of Sedona. He is a Pastoral Care Associate of Aria - Frankford Hospital. He taught at the National Academy of Massage Therapy and Health Sciences.

Rev. Mike was a faculty member of the Medical Mission Sister's Center for Human Integration's School of Integrated Body/Mind Therapies in Fox Chase, Philadelphia, PA for twelve years.

Rev. Mike is licensed by the teaching of Intuitional Metaphysics to practice Spiritual Healing and Scientific Prayer. Mike is also a Prayer therapist.

Rev. Mike was elected in 2007 to the status of "Fellow of the American Institute of Stress."

In 2008, Rev. Mike became a practitioner of Coincidental Recognition as he incorporated the CoRe system in to his spiritual healing practice.

In 2009, Rev. Mike trademarked a new healing process called Quantum Quatro! Subtle Energy System Support®.
In 2011, Rev. Mike joined the outreach program known as the Health Advantage Group.

In 2012, Rev. Mike became a Certified Professional Coach by The Master Coaching Academy and Joined The Personal Empowerment Group.

Prior to his metaphysical, ministerial and coaching studies, Rev. Mike worked for Sears Roebuck and Co. while in High School and after graduation until he joined the U. S. Air Force in 1965. He returned to Sears from Vietnam in 1969 and stayed until 1978. His final Sears assignment was as an efficiency expert in Methods - Operational Research and Development.

He volunteered with Burholme Emergency Medical Services from 1969 and is still a Life Member and Board of Directors Member. He started a private ambulance company in 1975 and worked professionally in the field until 2001 when he devoted his full attention to real estate investing, healing, coaching and writing.

www.ReverendMikeWanner.com

www.ingramcontent.com/pod-product-compliance
Lightning Source LLC
Chambersburg PA
CBHW061237180526
45170CB00003B/1343